Greece

JIM WESTCOTT

MEDIA ENHANCED BOOKS
AV2 BY WEIGL
ADDED VALUE • AUDIO VISUAL

www.av2books.com

AV² provides enriched content that supplements and complements this book. Weigl's AV² books strive to create inspired learning and engage young minds in a total learning experience.

Your AV² Media Enhanced books come alive with...

Audio
Listen to sections of the book read aloud.

Key Words
Study vocabulary, and complete a matching word activity.

Video
Watch informative video clips.

Quizzes
Test your knowledge.

Embedded Weblinks
Gain additional information for research.

Slide Show
View images and captions, and prepare a presentation.

Try This!
Complete activities and hands-on experiments.

... and much, much more!

Go to **www.av2books.com**, and enter this book's unique code.

BOOK CODE

A V Q 7 9 5 3 7

AV² by Weigl brings you media enhanced books that support active learning.

Published by AV² by Weigl
350 5ᵗʰ Avenue, 59ᵗʰ Floor
New York, NY 10118
Website: www.av2books.com

Library of Congress Cataloging-in-Publication Data

Names: Westcott, Jim, author.
Title: Greece / Jim Westcott.
Description: New York, NY : AV2 by Weigl, [2019] | Series: Exploring
  countries | Includes index. | Audience: Grades 4-6.
Identifiers: LCCN 2017055789 (print) | LCCN 2017058074 (ebook) | ISBN
  9781489675170 (Multi User ebook) | ISBN 9781489675163 (hardcover : alk.
  paper) | ISBN 9781489681621 (softcover ; alk. paper)
Subjects: LCSH: Greece--Juvenile literature.
Classification: LCC DF717 (ebook) | LCC DF717 .W37 2019 (print) | DDC
  949.5--dc23
LC record available at https://lccn.loc.gov/2017055789

Printed in the United States of America in Brainerd, Minnesota
1 2 3 4 5 6 7 8 9 22 21 20 19 18

032018
120817

Project Coordinator Heather Kissock
Art Director Terry Paulhus

Photo Credits
Every reasonable effort has been made to trace ownership and to obtain permission to reprint copyright material. The publishers would be pleased to have any errors or omissions brought to their attention so that they may be corrected in subsequent printings.

Weigl acknowledges Getty Images, Alamy, Newscom, and Shutterstock as its primary photo suppliers for this title.

Contents

Greece Overview

Greece is a country in southeastern Europe. The nation includes a peninsula that extends into the Mediterranean Sea, as well as thousands of islands. Greece has a long and rich history. Ancient civilizations made advances in science, art and literature, mathematics, and government that have influenced developments in these fields ever since. Today, millions of people visit Greece each year to enjoy its natural beauty, ancient monuments, and modern attractions.

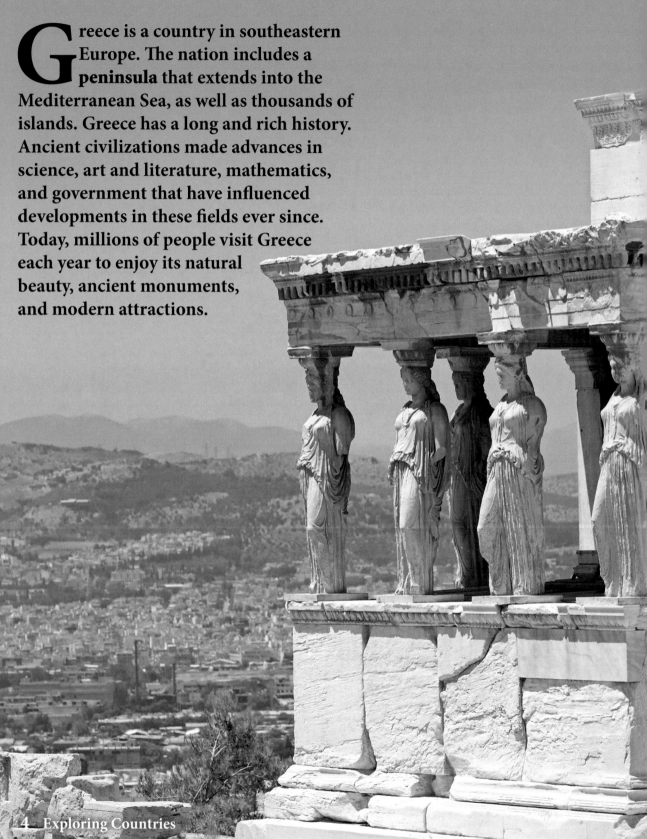

Steady breezes make windsurfing a popular sport for Greek islands residents and visitors.

Farmers throughout Greece grow olive trees. Olive oil is one of the country's leading agricultural products.

Baklava is a popular Greek dessert that includes thin layers of dough, chopped nuts, and honey.

Beautifully painted amphoras, or jars, created in ancient Greece are displayed in museums around the world.

Greece has a mild climate, allowing many people to enjoy dining outdoors.

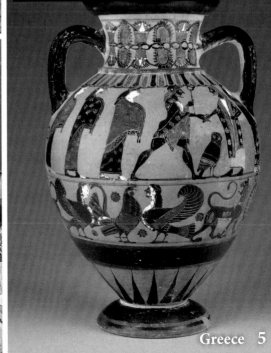

Exploring *Greece*

Greece covers an area of 50,949 square miles (131,957 square kilometers) and has 8,500 miles (13,675 km) of coastline. The country has land borders with Albania, Macedonia, and Bulgaria to the north and Turkey to the northeast. Three small seas that are part of the Mediterranean surround the Greek peninsula. To the west, the Ionian Sea separates Greece from southern Italy. The Sea of Crete is to the south, between the mainland and Crete, Greece's largest island. To the east, the Aegean Sea lies between Greece and Turkey.

Italy

Mount Olympus

Athens

Ionian Sea

N

Peloponnese

Mediterranean Sea

Map Legend

🗺 Greece	🐑 Peloponnese	📍 Capital City
📍 Land	▲ Mount Olympus	SCALE
〰 Water	🌙 Santorini	250 Miles / 250 Kilometers

Peloponnese

The Peloponnese is the region that is farthest south on the Greek peninsula. It is connected to the rest of the mainland by the **Isthmus** of Corinth. The Corinth ship canal now cuts across the isthmus.

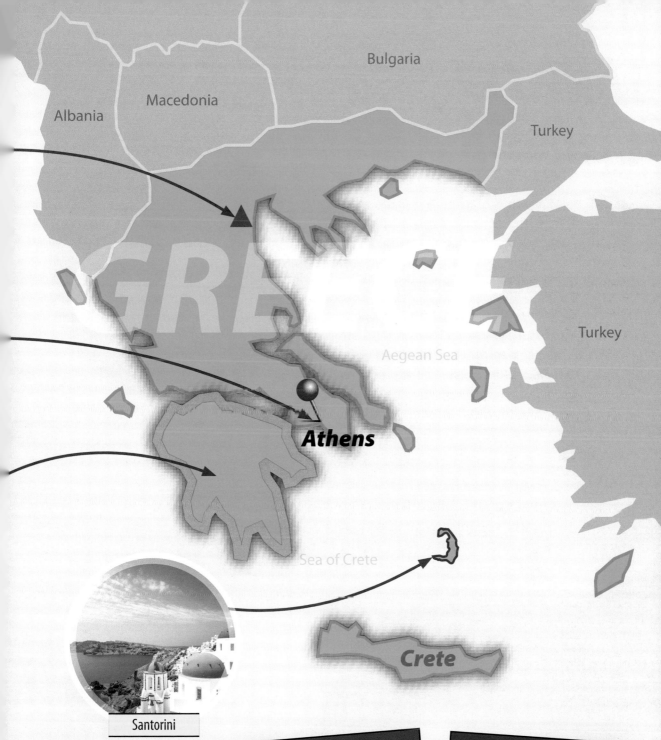

Albania

Macedonia

Bulgaria

Turkey

Turkey

GREECE

Aegean Sea

Athens

Sea of Crete

Crete

Santorini

Mount Olympus

Mount Olympus, in northern Greece, is the country's highest mountain. It stands 9,570 feet (2,915 meters) tall. Ancient Greeks believed Mount Olympus was the home of the gods that they worshipped.

Athens

Athens, the capital city, is in the region of Attica on the Greek peninsula. A settlement has existed on the site of present-day Athens for more than 5,000 years. Today, about 3 million people live in and around Athens.

Santorini

The island of Santorini, also called Thera, sits on a volcano. The island's area of 29 square miles (76 sq. km) is much smaller than in the past. A powerful volcanic eruption about 3,500 years ago caused the western half of Santorini to fall into the sea.

LAND AND CLIMATE

Greece is a mountainous country. About 80 percent of the land is mountain peaks or rocky areas at high **elevation**. A series of mountain ranges extend from north to south through mainland Greece.

The Pindus Mountains, which run through the center of the country, stretch from Albania to the Peloponnese. A number of peaks are more than 8,000 feet (2,440 m) tall. The mountains receive a great deal of rainfall. Many of Greece's rivers begin in the Pindus Mountains and flow either west to the Ionian Sea or east to the Aegean Sea.

The island of Nisyros was formed by a volcano that is still active, or capable of erupting again.

Valleys between mountain ranges or lowland areas near the coast make up the other 20 percent of Greece's land. Most of the country's people live in these lowland regions. The lowland areas also contain Greece's most **fertile** soil.

The Greek islands are well known for their beauty. Many islands have white-sand beaches, caves, and rocky cliffs that provide views of the sea. Clear, blue-green water surrounds most islands.

Many of Greece's islands were formed by volcanoes. Lava, or melted rock, that flows out of a volcano during eruptions can build up new land over time. Southern Greece lies slightly north of the border between two of Earth's **tectonic plates**. Often, volcanoes are common near plate borders. Another plate border that extends east–west across the mainland causes the major earthquakes that sometimes strike Greece.

From April to November, most of Greece has a hot and dry climate. A wind from the north called the Meltemi provides some relief from the heat, and temperatures are cooler at higher elevations. Winters are mild, and most of Greece's rainfalls occurs in the winter. The taller mountains on the mainland usually receive snow during the winter months.

The Vikos Gorge, a narrow canyon in the northern Pindus Mountains, is 1,600 feet (490 m) deep in places.

185 Miles
Length of the Haliacmon River, the longest river that is entirely in Greece. (300 km)

38 Square Miles
Area of Lake Trichonida, Greece's largest lake. (98 sq. km)

More Than 2,000
Number of Greek islands.

About 170
Islands on which people live.

PLANTS AND ANIMALS

One-half Portion of Greece's land on which maquis, a low shrub, can grow well.

A wide variety of plants are found in Greece. In the mountains, especially in northern Greece, **coniferous** trees such as firs and black pines grow at the highest elevations. Trees found on lower mountain slopes and in lowlands include poplars, oaks, plane trees, and various types of pines. Some kinds of trees and shrubs widespread in southern Greece are juniper, oleander, and maquis. In mountain valleys and other lowlands, many kinds of colorful flowers bloom each spring.

Animals that live in the mountains and other areas of northern Greece include Eurasian brown bears, deer, and martens. Some animals, such as wolves and wild boars, have become rare as a result of hunting and the growth of human settlements. Hares, porcupines, and wild goats thrive in southern Greece.

ABOUT 6,000 Number of species, or types, of flowers that grow in nature in Greece.

Pelicans, storks, herons, and owls are among the types of birds commonly seen in Greece. Reptiles include the **endangered** Cyclades blunt-nosed viper. This **venomous** snake lives on Milos and several other Greek islands.

3,000 Number of Cyclades blunt-nosed vipers living on the Greek islands.

Most Eurasian brown bears weigh between 300 and 550 pounds (135 and 250 kilograms).

NATURAL RESOURCES

G reece is not rich in natural resources. Only a few minerals are mined. Bauxite, used to make aluminum, is one of the country's leading mineral products. Another major product is marble. Polished Greek marble is used in the construction industry worldwide, especially for kitchen and bathroom fixtures.

Although only a small portion of the land has fertile soil, this land is an important resource for the country's agriculture industry. Leading crops include wheat, corn, cotton, fruits, vegetables, and olives, which are mostly used to make olive oil. Olive trees can grow well in a hot, dry climate and in rocky soil. Greece is the world's third-largest producer of olive oil.

Some land that cannot support crops is used to graze livestock. Cattle, sheep, and goats are raised for their milk, important to the country's dairy industry, as well as for their meat. Greece's rivers are used to produce **hydroelectricity**.

13% Portion of Greek workers with jobs in agriculture.

353,000 TONS Amount of olive oil Greece produced in 2016. (320,000 metric tons).

Almost 10% Portion of all the electricity used in Greece that comes from hydroelectricity.

Some marble quarries, or mines, on the island of Naxos have been used since at least the 7th century BC. The ancient Greeks created marble buildings and statues.

TOURISM

More than 25 million tourists visit Greece each year. Many visitors swim, sail, sunbathe, and walk the hill towns of the Greek islands. Some hike or climb in the country's mountains. Most tourists visit at least a few of Greece's **UNESCO** World Heritage Sites, to learn about the country's history and its artistic achievements.

The Monastiraki Flea Market is held every Sunday in Avissynias Square in the center of Athens.

Often, people traveling to Greece arrive in Athens. The city's many attractions include the Monastiraki Flea Market. Here, visitors can shop for carpets, jewelry, clothing, and a wide variety of collectibles. They can listen to street musicians and eat local foods.

The Acropolis is a hilltop World Heritage Site in Athens. During the 5th century BC, an Athenian leader named Pericles helped design and build temples on the Acropolis honoring Greek gods. The largest is the Parthenon, created to honor the goddess Athena. Athens is named after this goddess, and ancient Athenians believed she protected their city.

The Acropolis rises about 500 feet (150 m) above the rest of Athens. The word *acropolis* means "city at the top" in Greek.

Much of the Parthenon is still standing today. When it was built, the Parthenon contained a large statue of Athena. The statue, covered in gold and ivory, has been lost. The Erechtheum, another temple on the Acropolis, is well known for its caryatids. These are statues of female figures that serve as columns.

Northwest of Athens is Delphi, another World Heritage Site. Ancient Greeks believed Delphi was the center of the world. The ruins of a 4th-century BC temple honoring the god Apollo can be seen at Delphi. People from throughout ancient Greece would come to hear predictions from the oracle, a female priest, at the Delphi temple. She was believed to be speaking messages from Apollo. Next to the temple is a large theater that was also built in the 4th century BC.

Thessaloniki, Greece's second-largest city, shows the influence of many cultures at different periods in the country's history. The Arch of Galerius, built in the 3rd century AD when the Roman Empire ruled Greece, honors a military victory by the Emperor Galerius. The White Tower, built as a fort by Turkish rulers in the 1400s, is now a museum of the history of Thessaloniki.

INDUSTRY

Greece's manufacturing industries account for about 16 percent of the country's **gross domestic product** (GDP). Products manufactured in Greece include cement, chemicals, soap, and **textiles.** Cotton grown in Greece is used in the textile industry.

Many factories manufacture processed foods. These are ready-to-use food items made from the country's agricultural products. Food-processing factories make olive oil, fruit juice, and canned tomatoes.

Milk is used to manufacture a variety of dairy products, including cheese and yogurt. Often, the process used to make Greek yogurt results in a product that is creamier and less sweet than other kinds of yogurt. Greek yogurt is popular around the world. Well-known Greek cheeses include feta, graviera, kasseri, and kefalotyri.

15% Portion of Greek workers employed in manufacturing.

More Than **$300 Million**

Value of soap manufactured in Greece each year, much of it made using olive oil.

ONE-HALF

Fraction of all the cheese made in Greece that is feta.

Most factories manufacturing feta use both goat's milk and sheep's milk to produce the cheese.

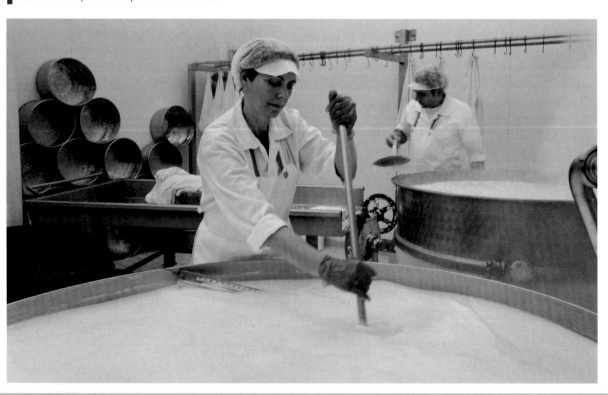

GOODS AND SERVICES

Greece trades with many nations. Products that it exports, or sells to other countries, include food, chemicals, and textiles. Greece imports, or buys from other nations, products such as machinery, transportation equipment, and fuels. In 1981, Greece joined the organization that later became the **European Union** (EU). Much of Greece's trade is with other EU countries.

More than 70 percent of Greek workers have service jobs. These people provide services to others rather than produce goods. Many service workers are employed in the tourism industry. They may work in hotels or museums. A large number of service jobs are with the government.

In recent decades, Greece's government borrowed hundreds of billions of dollars to help pay its expenses. By 2010, it no longer had enough money to make loan payments. The EU and other international organizations gave Greece new loans, but they required the government to reduce its employees, lower pensions to retired workers, and make other economic changes. For several years, Greece's annual GDP shrank, and the numbers of unemployed workers and people living in poverty increased. About one-third of people in Greece live in poverty.

$27 Billion Value of Greece's exports in 2016.

$45 Billion Amount of Greece's 2016 imports.

Almost $400 Billion Amount of loans to Greece from the EU and other organizations from 2010 to 2015.

24% Portion of Greek workers who were unemployed in 2016.

Some service workers operate the ferries and other ships that take visitors to many of the Greek islands.

INDIGENOUS PEOPLES

People have lived in Greece for thousands of years. In the 2000s BC, people on Crete known as the Minoans developed an advanced civilization. The Minoans built large palaces, had a written language, made decorated pottery and metal objects, and traded with other civilizations in the Mediterranean region. About 1600 BC, Minoan civilization was weakened by a series of disasters. These events included volcanic eruptions and earthquakes. Fires destroyed many Minoan palaces.

At about the same time, the Mycenaean civilization developed on mainland Greece. By 1400 BC, the Mycenaeans had conquered Crete. Mycenaean civilization lasted until about 1100 BC. Then, a people known as the Dorians conquered most of Greece.

The period of Dorian rule is often called the Dark Ages of Greek history. Civilization became less advanced. By the 9th century BC, Dorian control weakened. A number of Greek **city-states** developed, including Thebes, Corinth, Athens, and Sparta.

1900

Year that British **archaeologist** Arthur Evans began to uncover the ruins of Knossos, the Minoan civilization's capital city.

More Than 11,000

Number of objects, including Mycenaean gold jewelry, on display at the National Archaeological Museum in Athens.

13th or 12th Century BC

Time period when, according to Greek legends, Mycenaean King Agamemnon and other Greek leaders fought a war, known as the Trojan War, against the city-state of Troy, in Turkey.

Rooms in Minoan palaces, including the palace in Knossos, were decorated with frescoes, or artworks painted into plaster walls. Some paintings showed dolphins or other animals.

THE GREEK CITY-STATES

Over time, the Greek city-states became more powerful and developed advanced cultures. People from a number of city-states established new settlements around the Mediterranean. Through these settlements, Greek culture spread to other areas, including North Africa, southern Italy, and southern France.

Athens and Sparta reached the height of their achievements in the 5th century BC. Athenian **philosophers** Socrates and Plato, as well as the physician Hippocrates, advanced human knowledge. Athens is called the birthplace of democracy because it developed a system of government in which citizens made decisions about how they were ruled. Located in the Peloponnese, Sparta developed a strong military tradition. Beginning at age 7, boys lived away from their families, training to be soldiers.

From 431 to 404 BC, Athens and Sparta fought against each other in the Peloponnesian War. Sparta won, but both city-states became weaker. Starting in 358 BC, Philip II of the kingdom of Macedonia, in northern Greece, conquered the rest of the country. His son, known as Alexander the Great, built an empire extending from India in the east to Egypt and Libya in the west. His empire began to break up after Alexander died.

570 BC Year that Pythagoras, who made major advances in mathematics, was born on the Greek island of Samos.

300 Number of Spartan soldiers, led by King Leonidas, who fought to the death at the Battle of Thermopylae in 480 BC trying to stop an invading Persian army.

33 Years Old
Age of Alexander the Great when he died in 323 BC.

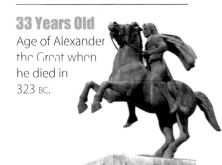

The ruins of a temple honoring Apollo can be seen at Syracuse, one of several ancient Greek settlements on the Italian island of Sicily.

FOREIGN RULE AND INDEPENDENCE

B y 146 BC, ancient Rome had conquered Greece. Many achievements of Roman civilization grew out of earlier advances made by the ancient Greeks in areas such as science, medicine, art, and **architecture**. By AD 285, the Roman Empire had grown so large that it was divided into western and eastern parts. Greece was in the eastern empire. It was governed from the city of Byzantium, which was renamed Constantinople in AD 330 by Emperor Constantine I. Today, this is the city of Istanbul, Turkey.

In 44 BC, Roman leader Julius Caesar created a new town at Corinth, 102 years after a Roman army had destroyed the city after the Battle of Corinth.

The western empire came to an end when German invaders conquered Rome in AD 476. The eastern part became known as the Byzantine Empire. In the 1200s, during the **Crusades**, much of Greece came under the control of Western European rulers. Western European control of some areas continued in the 1300s and 1400s.

European Crusaders built forts and castles to protect areas of Greece that they conquered. On the island of Rhodes, Crusaders expanded an old Byzantine fort to create the Palace of the Grand Master.

Also in the 1400s, the Ottomans expanded their empire. They were peoples from central Turkey. Ottoman Turks captured Constantinople, ending the Byzantine Empire. Greece became part of the Ottoman Empire, and Ottoman rule continued for almost 400 years.

By the 1800s, the Ottoman Empire had become weaker, and many Greeks wanted to govern themselves. Beginning in 1821, Greece fought a decade-long war for independence. The 1832 Treaty of Constantinople, in which the Ottoman Empire recognized Greece's freedom, officially ended the war. Greece became an independent kingdom.

In 1940, during World War II, German and Italian forces invaded Greece. They were driven out in 1944. Beginning in 1967, Greek military leaders controlled the government for several years. Greece adopted its current **constitution** in 1975. Under this document, Greece became a **republic**. The country no longer has a king or queen.

Cities in Greece hold parades to celebrate Independence Day on March 25. On that date in 1821, a revolt against Turkish rule began in the Peloponnese.

More Than 25,000

Number of Roman soldiers who defeated about 15,000 Greek troops at the Battle of Corinth in 146 BC.

1453

Year Mehmed II, the ruler of the Ottoman Empire, conquered Constantinople.

1974 Year that military rule ended in Greece.

POPULATION

Almost 11 million people live in Greece. The country is densely populated. This means it has, on average, more residents per square mile (sq. km) than many other nations. Greece has 216 people per square mile (83 per sq. km), compared to 92 people per square mile (35 per sq. km) in the United States.

More than three-fourths of Greece's population lives in **urban** areas. Three out of every ten people in the country live in and around Athens. Thessaloniki has 732,000 residents.

Greece's population is not growing. Many families have few children. In 2017, there were eight births per 1,000 people. Greece has a lower birth rate than almost every other country in the world.

In recent years, large number of **migrants** from the Middle East and Africa have come to Greece. Many of these people were trying to escape from wars or extreme poverty. Most migrants move on to other countries in Europe, but the Greek government and other groups have provided temporary homes, medical care, and other aid to new arrivals.

85th Greece's rank among nations of the world in population size.

81 How many years, on average, a child born in Greece can expect to live, a longer life span than in most other countries.

More Than 1 Million
Number of migrants reaching Greece in 2015–2016.

Many recent migrants to Greece arrived on the island of Lesbos after a risky journey in small, crowded boats.

POLITICS AND GOVERNMENT

U nder Greece's 1975 constitution, the president is the head of state. Greece's Hellenic Parliament, or legislature, elects the president. He or she serves a five-year term and has limited powers.

Members of the Hellenic Parliament are elected by the people. Legislative elections must be held at least once every four years. Often, the leader of the political party with the largest number of seats in the legislature is named by the president to be prime minister.

The prime minister is the most powerful government leader. He or she works with the legislature to pass new laws. The prime minister appoints cabinet ministers to provide advice and to be responsible for different areas of government, such as education or health.

Greece's legal system is based on ancient Roman law. The country's highest court is the Supreme Civil and Criminal Court. It has 56 judges.

17 Years Old
Age at which Greek citizens are required to vote in elections.

300 Number of members in the Hellenic Parliament.

1978
Year that Greece began using its current flag.

The Hellenic Parliament meets in a former palace, built in Athens during the 19th century for the king of Greece.

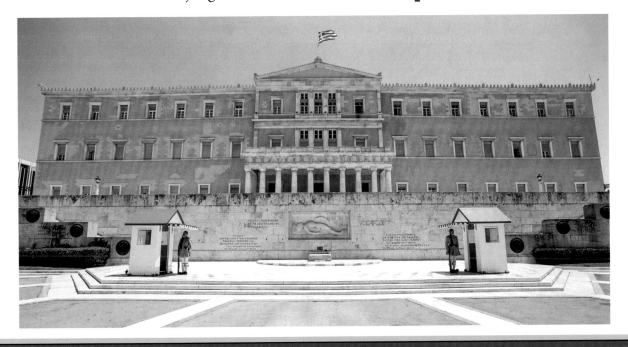

CULTURAL GROUPS

About nine out of ten people in Greece have Greek **ancestry**. The country's official language is Greek. It is written using an alphabet developed in about 1000 BC. Many people in Greece also learn English.

Members of other cultural groups have migrated to Greece over the centuries. Each of these groups contributes to Greek culture today. Albanians make up the second-largest cultural group in Greece. This cultural group includes the Cham Albanians and Arvanites. They arrived in Greece at different times and spoke different languages.

About 200,000 people in Greece are members of the Roma, or Romany, cultural group. This group, which originated in northern India, has a tradition of migration. Over the centuries, many Roma have moved to Greece and other European countries. Traditionally, Roma have often earned their living as musicians.

Νοσοκομείο Hospital 1 →
Αστυνομία Police 0,5 →
Μπόχαλη Mpohali 3 →
Πλάνος Planos 7 →
Τραγάκι 9
aki

Road signs in Greece are often written in both Greek and English.

Thousands of Albanian people from the Kosovo region came to Greece in the late 1990s to escape a war in their homeland.

Members of the Aromanian, or Vlach, cultural group live in several countries of southeastern Europe, including Greece. Many speak the Aromanian language. Some Aromanians celebrate the Koleda, or Koliada, festival each year in late December. As part of this festival, people gather in town squares for singing and dancing.

The Pomaks are members of a cultural group that originated in Bulgaria. Often, they speak the Pomak language, as well as Greek. Traditional Pomak wedding celebrations continue for two days. Everyone living in the bride and groom's home town may be invited. Often, the bride's face is painted white.

Most people in Greece are Christians. In the early 300s, Constantine I made Christianity the official religion of the Roman Empire, including Greece. Over time, differences developed between church leaders in the Byzantine Empire and the pope, or head of the Catholic Church in Rome. In the 11th century, the head of the church in Constantinople decided to completely separate from the Roman Catholic Church, establishing the Eastern Orthodox Church. The Eastern Orthodox, or Greek Orthodox, faith is now the official religion of Greece. About 1 percent of Greeks are Muslims, or followers of the religion Islam.

ABOUT 450,000
Number of people in Greece with Albanian ancestry.

1054 Year of the schism, or official separation, of the Roman Catholic and Eastern Orthodox faiths.

98%

Portion of Greeks who belong to the Eastern Orthodox Church.

Throughout the country, Greek Orthodox priests lead processions, or marches, in the days before the Easter holiday.

ARTS AND ENTERTAINMENT

The achievements of Greek creative artists date back thousands of years and continue in the present day. Ancient Greek writers have influenced many later authors. The works of these writers are still read and performed.

The poet Homer lived in the 9th or 8th century BC. He is believed to be the author of the **epic** poems *The Iliad* and *The Odyssey*. *The Iliad* is about the Trojan War. *The Odyssey* describes the adventures of the warrior Odysseus on his long journey home from the war. In the 7th century BC, the poet Hesiod's epic *Theogony* told stories about the origins of the Greek gods.

In 5th-century BC Athens, authors including Aeschylus, Sophocles, and Euripides wrote **dramas** about people's actions toward one another and why people behave as they do. Ancient Greek writers were the first to introduce **dialogue** into plays. Acting became a major art form and source of entertainment in ancient Greek theater.

Little is known about Homer's life. He may have lived in a Greek settlement on the Turkish coast.

Hesiod wrote the myth, or imagined story, of Pandora. The story relays how Pandora opened a box or jar, although told not to by the god Zeus. This allowed evil to enter the world. Many paintings over the centuries show the story of Pandora.

Outdoor theaters were built throughout ancient Greece, including the theater at Delphi and a larger one at Epidaurus in the Peloponnese. Many of the theaters that still exist are used today for plays, concerts, operas, and ballets. The Athens and Epidaurus Festival, held each year since 1955, uses both modern and ancient theaters for dance, music, and dramatic performances.

Greek creative artists of the 20th and 21st centuries include the composer and musician Yanni. His music combines several styles, such as classical, jazz, and rock. Yanni's recordings have sold millions of copies. Greek-born artist Lucas Samaras has created paintings, sculptures, and photographs. Many of his photos present distorted images, rather than showing the way people and objects really look.

Greece's film industry has produced talented directors and actors. The movies of Greek-born director Costa-Gavras often are based on political events. His 1969 film *Z* is about the murder of a fictional Greek politician by military officers. *Z* won an Academy Award for best foreign-language film. Greek-born actors Irene Papas, who starred in *Z*, and Melina Mercouri made films and won awards in both Europe and North America.

Arts and Entertainment BY THE NUMBERS

10 YEARS Length of Odysseus's journey and adventures in *The Odyssey*.

14,000 Number of people the Epidaurus theater seats.

1981 Year when Melina Mercouri became the minister of culture in Greece's government.

Yanni has given concert performances in cities all over the world, including Philadelphia in 2014.

SPORTS

From ancient to modern times, sports have been important to people in Greece. The Olympic Games originated in Greece. From the 8th century BC to the 4th century AD, the Games were held every four years at Olympia, in the Peloponnese. The original purpose of the Games was to honor Zeus. The first Olympics included only one event, a footrace. Over time, other events were added, including races of different distances, wrestling, and the long jump.

After more than 1,500 years, the Olympic Games were started again in 1896. The first modern Olympics were held in Athens. The city also hosted the Games in 2004.

At the 1896 Games, runner Spyridon Louis of Greece won the first modern Olympic marathon. The race is 26.2 miles (42.2 km) long, the distance from Marathon to Athens in ancient Greece. Louis's winning time was 2 hours, 58 minutes, and 50 seconds. Other Greek athletes who have won Olympic medals include weightlifter Pyrros Dimas. He won gold medals at the 1992, 1996, and 2000 Games, as well as a bronze medal at the 2004 Olympics.

Spyridon Louis received a silver cup for winning the 1896 Olympic marathon.

At the 2004 Olympics, Pyrros Dimas lifted a total of 337.5 kilograms (832.25 pounds) to win his bronze medal.

Mirela Maniani won two Olympic medals for Greece competing in the **javelin** throw, a silver medal at the 2000 Games and a bronze medal in 2004. At the 2016 Games, Anna Korakaki became the first Greek woman to win two medals at the same Olympics, with gold and bronze medals in shooting events.

Millions of Greeks enjoy playing and watching soccer, which is called football in Greece. Men's and women's national teams represent the country in international competitions. The men's team reached the **FIFA** World Cup tournament in 1994, 2010, and 2014. The World Cup is the highest-level international soccer competition. In 2004, the Greek men's team won the Union of European Football Associations' UEFA Euro tournament.

Basketball is also a popular sport in Greece. The men's and women's national teams compete in tournaments organized by the International Basketball Federation, known as FIBA. In 1987 and 2005, the men's team won FIBA's EuroBasket tournament, which determines the best team in Europe.

Eleni Daniilidou is one of Greece's top tennis players. She has won five singles championships and three doubles titles at Women's Tennis Association tournaments. Beach volleyball players Vassiliki Arvaniti and Vasso Karadassiou won gold medals in that sport at the 2005 and 2007 European women's championships.

Through 2017, Eleni Daniilidou had won about $3 million in prize money at tennis tournaments.

Sports BY THE NUMBERS

776 BC Year of the first Olympic Games in ancient Greece.

20 Years Old

Anna Korakaki's age when she won two Olympic medals at the 2016 Games.

#1 Vasso Karadassiou's ranking in 2005 among all women players by the European Volleyball Confederation.

Mapping Greece

W e use many tools to interpret maps and to understand the locations of
features such as cities, states, lakes, and rivers. The map below has many
tools to help interpret information on the map of Greece.

Map of Greece

Black Sea

Bosporus

Haliacmon River

• Thessaloniki
▲ Mount Olympus

40°N   40°N

Dardanelles

Lake Trichonida

Aegean Sea

Corinth •   ★ **Athens**

Ionian Sea

Isthmus of Corinth

36°N   36°N

Sea of Crete

• Heraklion
CRETE

20°E   24°E   28°E

Mediterranean Sea

MAP LEGEND

★ Capital City   ⌇ River   ╲ Longitude & Latitude
● City   -·-·- Country Border   ▢ Greece
⌇ Body of Water   ▲ Mountain   ▢ Other Countries

N
W   E
S

SCALE
0   100 Miles

0   100 Kilometers

Mapping Tools

- The compass rose shows north, south, east, and west. The points in-between represent northeast, northwest, southeast, and southwest.
- The map scale shows that the distances on a map represent much longer distances in real life. If you measure the distance between objects on a map, you can use the map scale to calculate the actual distance in miles or kilometers between those two points.

- The lines of latitude and longitude are long lines that appear on maps. The lines of latitude run east to west and measure how far north or south of the equator a place is located. The lines of longitude run north to south and measure how far east or west of the Prime Meridian a place is located. A location on a map can be found by using the two numbers where latitude and longitude meet. This number is called a coordinate and is written using degrees and direction. For example, the city of Athens would be found at 38°N and 24°E on a map.

Map It!

Using the map and the appropriate tools, complete the activities below.

Locating with latitude and longitude

1. Which city is found at 41°N and 23°E?
2. What mountain is located at 41°N and 22°E?
3. Which isthmus is found on the map using the coordinates 38°N and 23°E?

Distances between points

4. Using the map scale and a ruler, calculate the approximate distance between the cities of Athens and Heraklion, Crete.
5. Using the map scale and a ruler, calculate the approximate distance between Thessaloniki and Athens.
6. Using the map scale and a ruler, calculate the approximate east–west length of the island of Crete.

ANSWERS 1. Thessaloniki 2. Mount Olympus 3. Isthmus of Corinth 4. 200 miles (320 km) 5. 190 miles (305 km) 6. 160 miles (260 km)

Quiz Time

Test your knowledge of Greece by answering these questions.

1 What is the capital of Greece?

2 What region of Greece is farthest south on the Greek peninsula?

3 Which three seas surround the Greek peninsula?

4 What is the name of the largest Greek island?

5 What is the longest river located entirely in Greece?

6 What temple on the Acropolis honored Athena?

7 In what year were the first ancient Olympics held?

8 What is the name of Homer's epic poem about the Trojan War?

9 On what date do Greeks celebrate Independence Day?

10 What is the official religion of Greece?

ANSWERS

1. Athens
2. The Peloponnese
3. The Ionian Sea, Sea of Crete, and Aegean Sea
4. Crete
5. The Haliacmon River
6. The Parthenon
7. 776 BC
8. *The Iliad*
9. March 25
10. The Eastern Orthodox, or Greek Orthodox, faith

Key Words

ancestry: referring to people in one's family or cultural group in past times

archaeologist: a scientist who studies ancient peoples and civilizations

architecture: the styles in which buildings are designed

city-states: independent states that include a city and the surrounding land

coniferous: referring to trees and shrubs that have cones

constitution: a document establishing a country's form of government, the powers of the government, and the rights of the people

Crusades: a series of wars begun by European powers to gain control of land in the Middle East and other areas

dialogue: a conversation between two or more people, such as actors in a play

drama: plays that are about serious subjects and often involve some type of conflict

elevation: the height of an area of land above sea level

endangered: at risk of becoming extinct, or no longer surviving in the world

epic: a long poem, often describing the achievements of a legendary hero or historic figure

European Union: a political and economic organization, established in 1993, of more than two dozen countries

fertile: referring to land that is suitable for growing crops or other plants

FIFA: the Fédération Internationale de Football Association, which sets the rules for international soccer and organizes international tournaments

gross domestic product: the total value of all the goods and services produced in a country's economy

hydroelectricity: electricity produced using the energy in moving water, such as a flowing river

isthmus: a narrow strip of land that connects two larger areas of land

javelin: a long, thin metal spear that is thrown for distance in sports competitions

migrants: people who travel from one area to another, in order to live in the new location permanently or temporarily

peninsula: an area of land surrounded on three sides by water

philosophers: thinkers who develop theories about human behavior, beliefs, and ways of gaining knowledge

republic: a form of government in which the head of state is elected

tectonic plates: large sections of Earth's surface that are constantly moving very slowly

textiles: woven or knit fabrics

UNESCO: the United Nations Educational, Scientific, and Cultural Organization, whose main goals are to promote world peace and eliminate poverty through education, science, and culture

urban: related to cities and towns

venomous: referring to snakes that produce venom, a substance that can injure or kill people and other animals

Index

Log on to www.av2books.com

AV² by Weigl brings you media enhanced books that support active learning. Go to www.av2books.com, and enter the special code found on page 2 of this book. You will gain access to enriched and enhanced content that supplements and complements this book. Content includes video, audio, weblinks, quizzes, a slide show, and activities.

AV² Online Navigation

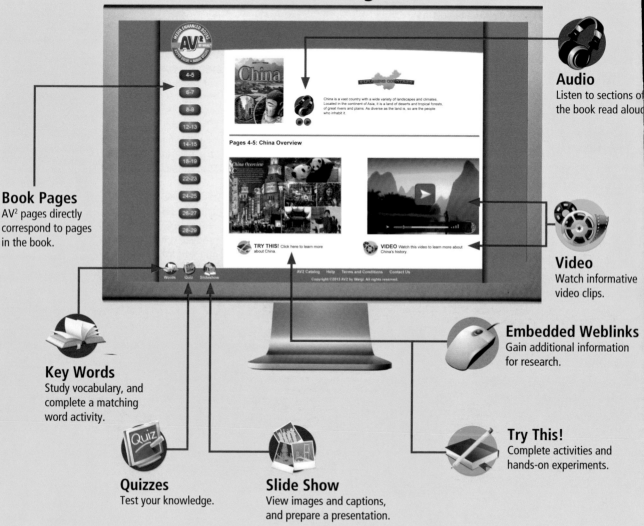

Book Pages
AV² pages directly correspond to pages in the book.

Audio
Listen to sections of the book read aloud.

Video
Watch informative video clips.

Key Words
Study vocabulary, and complete a matching word activity.

Quizzes
Test your knowledge.

Slide Show
View images and captions, and prepare a presentation.

Embedded Weblinks
Gain additional information for research.

Try This!
Complete activities and hands-on experiments.

AV² was built to bridge the gap between print and digital. We encourage you to tell us what you like and what you want to see in the future.

Sign up to be an AV² Ambassador at www.av2books.com/ambassador.